D1146104

NORFOLK

Loving it!

JOHN DUCKETT

HALSGROVE

First published in Great Britain in 2010

British Library Cataloguing-in-Publication Data
A CIP record for this title is available from the British Library

ISBN 978 0 85704 038 1

HALSGROVE
Halsgrove House,
Ryelands Industrial Estate,
Bagley Road, Wellington,
Somerset TA21 9PZ
Tel: 01823 653777
Fax: 01823 216796
email: sales@halsgrove.com

Part of the Halsgrove group of companies.
Information on all Halsgrove titles is available at: www.halsgrove.com

Printed and bound in China by
Toppan Leefung Printing Ltd

INTRODUCTION

NORFOLK - LOVING IT! is my third book containing fine art photographs of my beloved county of Norfolk, taken by me, Norfolk born landscape photographer John Duckett. Following the success of the first two books – *The Romantic Norfolk Coast* and *Romantic Norfolk*, I decided to challenge myself even more this time by photographing this beautifully produced collection of the county's landscape and seascape images largely in a panoramic format. It is easy to lose the dominance of the sky in this format and this is something I was determined not to allow to happen. As everyone knows Norfolk is famed for its huge skies and for me it was imperative to portray this in these images. My aim has been to capture the atmosphere and colours of both the stormy dramatic days and cold still dawns of winter, along with the beautiful evening light and sunsets of summer. I hope in many of the photographs in the book to have portrayed the amazing colours and light which can be found at either end of the day.

The book covers not only inland Norfolk with its wide open arable fields, gently meandering rivers, wonderful churches and of course the ancient peat diggings which today form the Broads, but also the diverse Norfolk coast with its sandy and shingle beaches, cliffs, salt marshes, dunes and creeks. As with my previous two books it was important to me to try and achieve a timeless quality to the images, so wherever possible I tried to stay clear of Norfolk's towns and villages where crowds and traffic intrude upon even the most picturesque urban scene. Instead I wanted to try and bring the reader a collection of images in which to lose themselves.

Over the years I have slowly developed what I feel is my unique atmospheric style through experience and experimentation with different camera settings and filters. I spent many years using 35mm SLR film cameras using various colour and black and white print films as well as transparencies. Over this time I learned the techniques of metering, balancing exposure with filters, depth of field and composition as well as, of course, working with the light. Once I had learned the basics I used this experience to achieve what I believe to be my unique style. My landscapes have the emphasis on drama. Wherever possible I try to steer clear of the typical bright and sunny shots so often seen. I love capturing atmosphere in my images and spend hours waiting for the right light conditions and clouds. Bright sunshine and blue skies are not generally for me, I much prefer to produce a dramatic moody image. In 2004 I made the conversion from film to digital SLR cameras. It took a while to adapt to this new technology but I was determined to use my experience of film, and still maintain to this day the importance of getting it right in the camera and not relying on the computer afterwards.

The panoramic photographs in this book are not formed from images stitched together on the computer but instead are photographs specifically composed to suit a panoramic format and then simply cropped. For me it remains important to try and preserve the traditional techniques of photography.

My interest in photography began back in my early teens whist on family holidays taken throughout the UK. My mum, Joan, had always been a keen photographer, so dad, Brian, and brother, Paul, were already quite used to spending much of their holiday waiting around for her to catch them up or stopping at every lay-by just in case there was a photograph to be had. This support and understanding really helped me in the earlier years and allowed me time to learn the importance of waiting for the right light conditions when taking landscape photographs. However it was not until quite recently that I started to turn my passion for landscape photography into a career. During 2004 I joined an on-line photography website and started to upload some of my images for the critique of others. On the whole my images went down really well and I started to realise that other people also liked my moodier take on landscape photography, not only my mum and Alison! From there I joined the Wymondham Photographic Society. It was there that I was encouraged to enter my images into their competitions and even a couple of small exhibitions. The images got a really good response and my confidence started to grow. After moving to north Norfolk it was just too far to travel to the club any longer and it was with regret that I had to leave. However, I will always be grateful for the confidence they gave me. In August 2005 I attended my first craft show at the Aylsham show in Norfolk. This was a great success and things started to take off. Now over five years later I am a semi-professional photographer. I've published three books, undertaken shows and exhibitions throughout Norfolk, and have work permanently for sale at galleries, regularly selling prints throughout the country and overseas from my website www.jduckettimages.co.uk. I've also undertaken commissions for use in advertising, have had work published in books, magazines, calendars and even produced a range of greetings cards for the National Trust at Blickling Hall.

I hope you enjoy this new book.

John Duckett
2010

The River Wensum on a cold and frosty winter's morning near Guist.

ACKNOWLEDGEMENTS & DEDICATION

I wish to dedicate this book to my wonderful son Oliver. I am sorry I wasn't able to spend as much time as I wanted with you during your first year, Ollie but I promise now this book is finally finished I'll try to be the best dad in the world for you.

I also again wish to dedicate this book to my darling wife Alison. With the birth of our son Oliver during the production of this book times have been difficult and days have been long. Without her constant patience, understanding and unwavering support this book would again never have made it to print.

The remains of a sandcastle is washed away by the incoming tide at Brancaster beach.

Happisburgh lighthouse bathed in the warmth of the late evening light.

Boats at high tide in the creek at Brancaster Staithe.

Looking across the dunes to the sun setting over Scoult Head Island near Burnham Overy Staithe.

The ruins of Castle Acre near Swaffham.

Solitary boat at Brancaster Staithe.

A stormy day at the seaside resort of Cromer.

Looking out across a snow-covered Wells beach to the distant dunes.

The shoreline at Holkham.

A pre-dawn shot of the quayside at Wells-next-the-Sea.

A winter's dawn at the white windmill of Thurne

Snow-covered trees across the lake in Blickling Park.

Cromer pier surrounded by the colours of dawn.

Brancaster beach at low tide.

A gap in the storm clouds reveals blue sky beyond the shingle bank at Cley-next-the-Sea.

Boats moored alongside Blakeney Quay.

A wave rushes inland towards the dunes on Holkham Beach.

Sunrise caught behind the old coastal defences at Happisburgh.

Waveforms, Happisburgh.

Bluebell woods in Blickling Park.

Dawn over the creek at Thornham.

Coastal defensive rocks on the beach at Happisburgh.

A line of clouds and the blue sky reflected in high tide water at Thornham

Field of Norfolk lavender near Heacham.

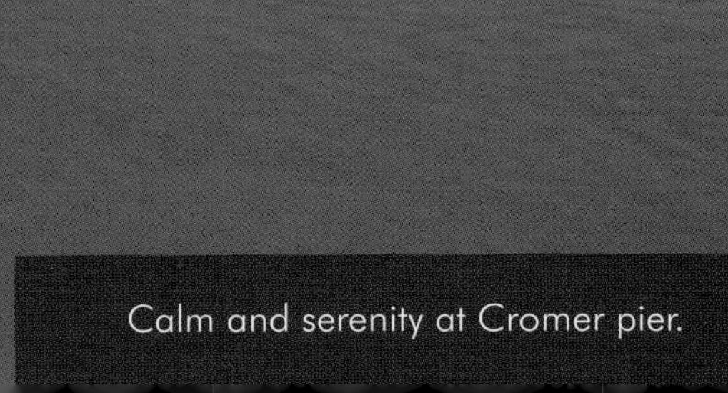

Calm and serenity at Cromer pier.

A misty morning near How Hill.

Field of barley in late summer.

Boat moored in the creek at Thornham.

Sunrise over the sea at Trimingham.

'Poppies & Post' – an image of Norfolk summer.

Dawn over the sea at Holkham.

Harvest time in north Norfolk.

Waves crash into the old sea defences at Happisburgh.

Windsock at Little Snoring airstrip.

Boats at low tide in the estuary at Morston.

JULIA
AMBER

Looking towards sunrise across the beach at Old Hunstanton.

A field of poppies near Fakenham.

The tops of a groyne stretches out to sea near East Runton.

The sky reflected in the expanse of water at Barton Broad.

A path through the dunes leads to the beach at Horsey Gap.

Posts which mark the mussel beds at Old Hunstanton.

Dusk at Sheringham.

The road leading to the church at Sharrington.

Hunstanton cliffs reflected in a pool left at low tide.

Cart Gap near Happisburgh.

Rocks exposed by the low tide at Sheringham.

The dunes at Wells-next-the-Sea reflected in the wet sand.

The remains of an old jetty at Thornham.

Sunrise over Salhouse Broad.

A pool on the salt marsh at Thornham.

'Boat & Barn' at Thornham.

Looking across the estuary at Wells-next-the-Sea towards the 'Island'.

Looking back towards land across the sea filled bowl at Holkham beach

A wave rolls ashore on to the shingle beach at Cley-next-the-Sea.

Palmer's Mill spinning in the wind near Upton Dyke.

The conservation centre on Ranworth Broad.

Sunrise at low tide, Morston.

Sunset turns to dusk over the calm waters at Brancaster Staithe.

A stormy sky reflected in Filby Broad.

The sun sets behind Cromer.

The River Bure near Alysham.

Beach huts at Wells-next-the-Sea.

Sunset over the salt marsh at Stiffkey.

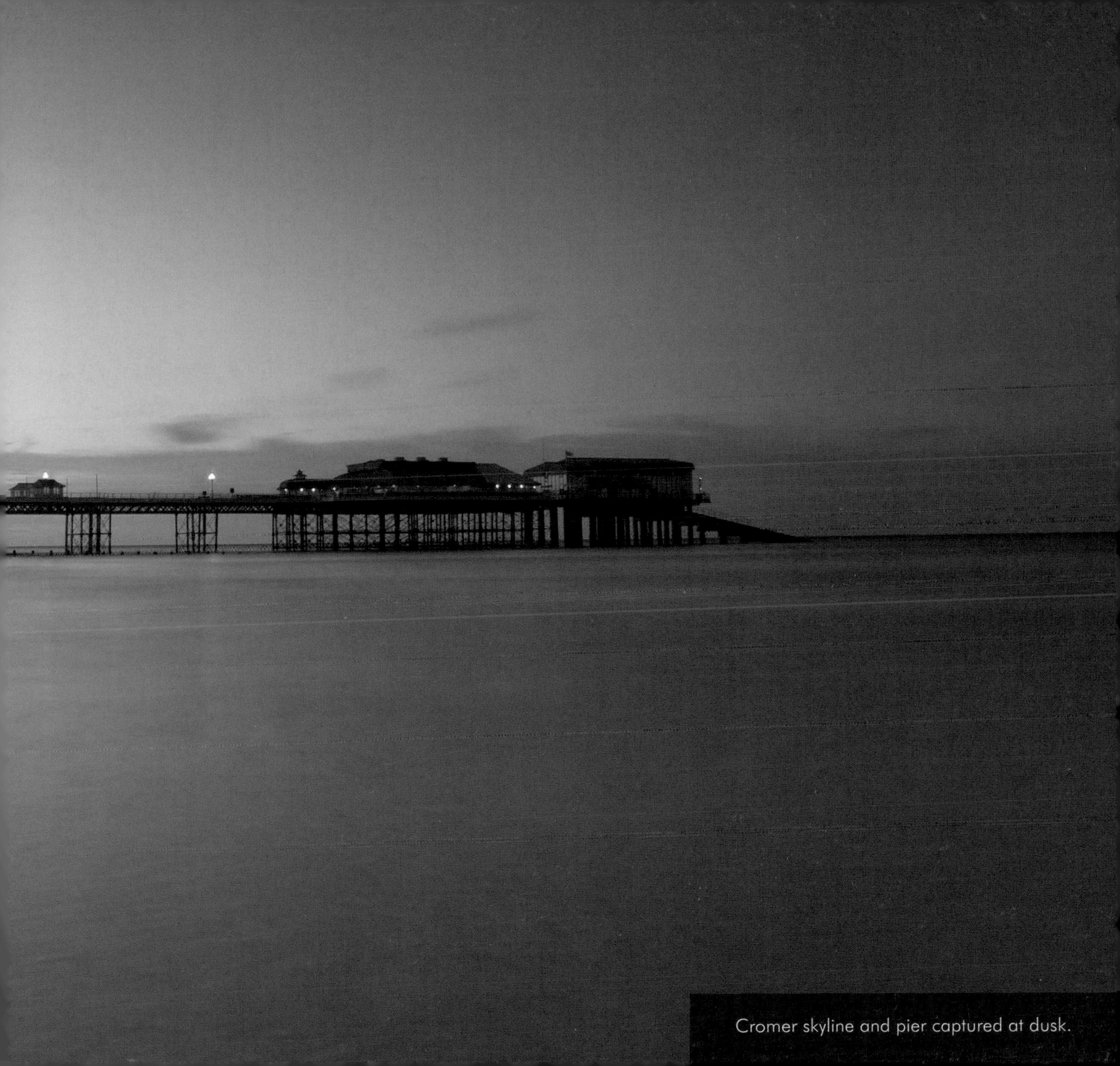

Cromer skyline and pier captured at dusk.

The tower of Salle church dominates the surrounding countryside.

The quayside at Blakeney.

LOVERS

Looking up at St Benet's wind pump near Ludham.

Moored boats in Upton Dyke.

A frosty morning on the river Wensum near Swanton Morley.

A storm approaches beyond the mussel beds at Brancaster Staithe.

Early morning mist starts to clear from this dyke in the Broads.

Dusk and high tide combine to give a serene picture at Brancaster Staithe.